C000162688

forever is just
a moment

Ginnie Bale

to M.

You inspired me to grow and write.

I write about you
to tell the world how well
you stole my heart,
and to let them know
how far it had to travel
to find its way back
home.

to my readers

You felt the pain
that comes with a broken heart
and still believe in love.

This book is for you.

SUMMER

laughing & loving

Hello Stranger,
I haven't even
touched your skin,
but you've already
touched my
 h e a r t.

I was longing
for freedom
and saw
the wild
in your
eyes.

My soul speaks
a language,
only you
can understand.

I pretended to be strong,
until you showed me
how beautiful
weakness
 looks on me.

You asked questions,
that no one ever asked
before.

And I told you secrets,
I've never told
anyone before.

I fell in love with the ocean,
the first time I looked
    into your eyes.

I was broken
into a million pieces
but you said
you like the
challenge
of a puzzle.

And you put me
back together
piece by piece;
to see the
big picture.

One day,
the thought of love
won't make me sad
anymore.

I hope it's
because of you.

I asked for a light
and the universe
sent a firework.

Ginnie Bale

They said
I can't have
everything,
but with you
I start to
believe
I can.

There are oceans between us,
yet we don't feel a distance.

I don't want you
to heal me.

All I'm asking for is
please don't break me,
for I'm already broken.

You taste like
f o r e v e r
and I'd like to
take one more sip.

When I stopped
believing in love
the universe
sent you
to remind me
that love,
true love,
does exist.

Even for me.

I will learn
a hundred
languages,

to tell you
in each one
how much
I adore you.

I'm in love with
the way you're
trying to hide
your *magic*
  from me.

You are the glue,
that holds my broken
pieces together.

You keep me from
 falling apart.

I see the calm in your eyes.
But your smile says,
it's only the calm
before the storm.

Let's call it love.

The feeling of
flying and drowning
at the same time.

Let's call it love
and

  d

     r

       o

          w

            n

                   in it.

You make me believe
in impossible things.

Like you and me
ending up
together.

When I fell in love
with you,
I fell in love
 with myself again.

I want you
to kiss me the
way a match
kisses paper —

to set it on fire.

Trying to describe you
is like trying to paint
a rainbow with
a pencil.

I might reflect
the shading
but never fully
catch the *colors*.

I told you *I'm fucked up*
and you smiled and said,

    "We're all a little
    fucked up, dear.
    And so is life."

With you,
I forget why
I built the walls
around my heart.

You see right through them.

I love every part of you
that I've known so far.

Even more do I love
the hidden parts
I have yet
to discover.

I want to drown
in your eyes
and live in
your soul
  forever.

I've never been
afraid of dying
until I met you.

Because with you,
for the first time
I had something
to lose.

Love is the ink
and you are
the pen
for my

p o e t r y.

Some feelings were
too much for me
to explain.

So, I kept quiet
for a while
 and just
  felt.

FALL

feeling & falling

I'm wondering
if this is the end
or the beginning
of us.

You made me feel again,
  now I'm feeling too much.

Loving you
is terrifying.

And I'm not sure
if I'm brave enough
to love you a
little longer.

You need to understand,
that I will never be
all yours.

There will always
be a part of me
that belongs
   to the

         w i l d.

Look at us.
Look what happens,
when two people
are too afraid
to love each
other.

The stars are proof
that we can feel
magic even from afar.

Can we
pretend
just a
little
longer
that
we
belong
together?

I've loved you
from the very
first moment.

But I still have
to figure out
how to love

    m y s e l f.

You deserve
all the love
I can't give
    to you.

Tell me you love me.
Tell me you'll stay.
Tell me everything
will be okay.
Lie to me.
Only this
one time.

I don't want to be
   your sunshine.

I want to be the rain,
when you're longing
   for *g r o w t h.*

You and I, we are
Venus and Mars,
fighting gravity,
trying to leave
our orbits,
just to come
a little closer
to each other for
a moment in time.

Please stay.
I'd like to waste
a little more
time on you.

I push you away,
when I want you to hold me.

I keep quiet,
when I want to tell you
how much you mean to me.

I watch you leave,
when I want to beg you to stay.

Hope is
killing me
and hope is
keeping me
alive.

I was afraid you might
break my heart;
so, I rather
broke it myself.

I want to be
your blanket,
on the days
you're trying
to hide from
 the world.

| Ginnie Bale

You were waiting
for three words
I never said
because
I knew,
three words
could never
express the
amount of *feelings*
I felt for you.

They say
follow your heart.

But my heart
crossed the ocean
and I'm afraid
to *drown*
in the waves.

I wish I could love
a little more
like you.

Like nobody
ever broke my heart.
Like I don't know the pain.
Like I'm not terrified of it.

For the blink of an eye
we dreamed of forever.

Blink.

Just because I found
the strength to
leave you,
doesn't mean
I'm strong enough
  to stay away.

My heart misses you
in thousand different ways.
Each one, an aching pain.

I lied to you.

I don't want you
in my life.
I want you
to be my life.

My heart is
too messy
to make it
a comfortable
home for you.

A place
where you'd
want to *stay*.

There are two hearts
beating in my chest.

One that wants you
to be with me and
one that wants you
to be happy.

I don't know if this
is what I want,
but it is what
I need right
   now.

Why am I so afraid
to love you,
when all I've ever
wanted was
a love like
  yours?

I was willing
to give you
all the broken
pieces but
you asked
for my
whole
heart.

| Ginnie Bale

'*I love you*'
is such an
underrated way
to say that I believe
the universe was
 only made for us
   to meet each other.

How could I ever be
mad at you for leaving,
when you first taught me
how to survive
on my own?

Just like your words,
    your silence was poetry.

Do you remember
when you said
you can't have me?

I was yours.
All this time.

You were looking for
light and laughter,
love and lust,
dancing and
dreaming.

But I was also
fighting and falling,
damaged and drowning,
hiding and hurting.

Our love language was silence,
and a subtle smile
at times.

| Ginnie Bale

You said;
*Never give up
on any dream.*

But what if
I'm dreaming
of you?

When we met
my heart whispered
f o r e v e r and
my head yelled
he will leave.

Late at night,
I listen to the trees.

They tell secrets about
the moon and the sun.
They've never met.

Just like you and me.

You loved
my broken
  pieces
more than I
ever could.

If I were *strong*,
I'd break my walls
and let you in.

If I were *brave*,
I'd tell you that
I love you.

If I were *clever*,
I'd never give up
on us.

If I were *someone else*,
I'd be with you.

I couldn't give you
all of me and
half of me wasn't
 enough for you.

I will write about
how much I miss you,
until you come back to me.

Then I will write about
how much I love you,
until the end of time.

If love is an illusion,
you were an
exceptional
magician.

Ginnie Bale

We say goodbye,
because we don't know
  how to spell

    f o r e v e r.

WINTER

drowning & darkness

Every day I'm trying
to let you go and
every day I fail
  once more.

Whenever I close my eyes
and go to my happy place,
you are already there.

Seasons come and go,
but my heart always
feels like winter
  without you.

Why are
hellos
so much
easier than

goodbyes?

forever is just a moment |

I'm trying to read
between the
l i n e s
of your silence.

My heart still
calls you
home.

Even though
you're long gone.

I hope you
didn't cry
over me,
because
I shed
enough
t e a r s
for both
 of us.

You loved me in a way,
that made me forget
 all the people
  who never did.

I felt *you*,
when I
failed
to feel
anything
at all.

All that's left
are broken promises
and dreams that will
never come true.

I knew you wouldn't come,
on that rainy day in February.
I knew you wouldn't come
but I waited until
the rain washed away
any bits of hope
I had left.

Just the way you loved me,
you broke my heart
    softly.

I cry tears over you
that you will never see,

write letters for you,
I will never send,

and sing songs about you,
hoping your heart
  might listen.

You smile but
your eyes tell me
e v e r y t h i n g
I need to know.

I don't know
where to search for
all the pieces of myself
  that I lost in you.

Our love was a symphony
in D minor.

I can't make
the darkness
disappear,

but I can
hold your hand,
so we won't get
lost in it.

I keep telling my heart
that you were not the one
but *it won't listen*.

Tonight I saw a
shooting star.

I wished for you
to come back to me
and you did.

I just forgot to wish
  for you to stay.

I miss you a little more
on the rainy days.

I was heartbroken
many times before.
But this time
felt different.

This time
my *soul* broke.

My favorite sound
is the echo of your words
resonating within the silence
   of your absence.

I didn't do anything
to keep you from leaving,
but I will do everything,
to keep myself from
falling apart (again).

Please be patient with me.

I'm still learning
how to *let go*.

Every night,
right before I fall asleep,
I close my eyes and
whisper your name,
hoping one day
you'll answer
and kiss me
good night.

| Ginnie Bale

I left reality
a long time ago,
searching for a place
 where we can
   meet again.

At times I wonder if
we found each other
at the wrong time.

But I know you
found me just in time
  to save me.

You left light,
where others
left darkness.

Your name on my heart
is written in heavy
l e t t e r s
and I can't carry
the weight anymore.

Ginnie Bale

We shared our
hopes and dreams,
  but we didn't share
    our fears.

I smile –
even on my
darkest days.

For you once said
it melts your heart.

I don't want to be the girl
who pushes people away.

I don't want to be the girl
who runs away.

I don't want to be the girl
who's afraid of love.

I want to be the girl
who is brave.

I want to be the girl
who s t a y s.

I want to be
your girl.

How can I let go,
when your silence

screams

my name?

Whenever my heart
starts healing,
you come back
for a little moment,
just to leave me
once again,
with open wounds.

As if they never
stopped bleeding
  at all.

H o p e
whispered
your name
and taught me
how to breathe
through the pain.

Ginnie Bale

Every night
I tell the moon
how much I miss you
    and he promises
    to tell you in
    your sleep.

Tears are raindrops
that wash away
the dirt from
 our *souls*.

Yesterday I was afraid
because nobody ever
loved me the way
you did.

Today I'm afraid
that nobody will ever
love me the same
way.

SPRING

hurting & healing

This is not a story
about happy endings,

       this is a story about
       new beginnings.

You and I belong
together.

Just not in this life.

There are things in life,
that are special because
they are rare.

Such as rainbows.
Shooting stars.

Y o u.

Ginnie Bale

I will wander around
until I find a place
where I miss you
   a little less.

Trust me, I've tried.
It is *impossible*
to forget a soul
that once kissed
  your heart.

| Ginnie Bale

You fade
like a sunset
and all that's left
is the memory of
a colorful sky.

I was a girl
searching for
dreams and
you were a boy,
looking for someone
you could share
your *dreams*
  with.

And we dreamed together,
until we woke up
  one day.

What if
we both
are waiting
for the other to
take the first step?

Love is not always
kisses and roses.

Sometimes,
love is two people
adoring each other,
but being afraid of
not being enough.

Sometimes,
love is admiring
someone from
a distance,
afraid to come
any closer.

Sometimes,
love is letting go,
hoping to meet
each other again
  some day.

I said I hope you're fine,
but what I meant was
I hope you find your way
back to me.

You and I,
we were a perfect balance
of fire and water.

Just the right amount of water
to keep the flame under control,
without taming the wild.

This is not
the end of the world.
Just the end of us.

But some days,
I can't see
the *difference.*

Last year we shared
the same dreams.

This year we share
nothing but memories.

I was tired of
begging people to stay
when they wanted
    to leave.

You only saw
  that I

p u s h e d you
  in the water,

but you didn't see
  that I was
    a sinking
      ship.

I asked
myself
again and
again
why
you left,

but I never
asked you
to stay.

There's a part of me
that will always love you

and there's a part of me
that is glad you left.

You were
everything
I dreamed of,
and everything
I thought I didn't
  deserve.

To be with you,
I had to walk out
of the shadows
and I wasn't ready
to illuminate my
    s c a r s.

I can't let you go all at once.
I let you go in pieces.

One piece
at a time.

It hurts a little less
this way.

I was broken
when we met
and broken
when you left
but I never felt
more *whole*
in between.

We can't rewrite the past.
So you'll forever be the boy
who loved me unconditionally,

       and I will forever be
       the girl who was afraid,
       to love you back.

I didn't let you in,
for there was
no room
for two
in the chaos
of my mind.

Maybe I will miss you
for the rest of my life
but I will miss you
without *hurting*
  (anymore).

Sometimes love finds us,
only to remind us
that we're still
able to
love.

You didn't leave me.
And I didn't leave you.

We were just tired of
pretending to be fine
 when we were not.

I've spent countless
nights
in the dark
watching the stars.

Tonight they shine
 a little brighter.

If I'm lucky,
you'll find your way
back to me
one day.

If you're lucky,
my heart will still
beat for you then.

And if we're both lucky,
incredibly lucky,
it would be the beginning
  of forever.

I needed a friend
far more than I needed
a lover.

And we both knew,
we could never be
just friends.

To find
peace,
I have to
forgive you
for leaving,
and I have to
forgive myself
for letting
 you go.

They don't understand
why I still can't let go
after all this time.

They don't know,
I meet you every night
  in my dreams.

We planted love
and forgot to water
the seeds.

The difference
between yesterday
and today is,
today I know
I don't need
   you to

         s u r v i v e.

| Ginnie Bale

I'm sorry
for all the things
I never said.

We were two
s t r a n g e r s,
who desperately
wanted to believe
that there is
something
good left
in this world.

So, we believed
in love.

I didn't lose you
because I was tired of
climbing the mountain.

        I lost you because
        I was afraid of
        the heights.

Oh, how much we
loved each other.

Only our definitions
of love were entirely
d i f f e r e n t.

Maybe we weren't
meant to be together
in this lifetime.

Maybe we were
only meant to meet,
to remind us
that soulmates do exist.

And maybe, just maybe,
that's enough for now.

I will always remember you,
when I see that one star
on the night sky,
shining a little
brighter than
the other
s t a r s.

I mistook a chapter for a book
and cried over an ending
that was supposed to be
    a new beginning.

In the end we both
found something.

I found myself and you
found someone new.

You are happy now
and I will be too.

Eventually.

Did you
save me,
or did I
save myself
because of
   you?

You will
always mean
something to me.

You will always be
my favorite
somefling.

I wonder
how many
lifetimes
it will take
my heart,
to forget the sound
of your heart
  beating for it.

You came into
my life,
to show me
what true love
feels like.

And you left,
to teach me
that I have to fight
for what I truly
want (to stay).

You wanted a love
that's loud and
I've loved you
quietly.
So, you left.
And I whispered

I love you,
goodbye.

I didn't mean
to hurt you.
But I didn't mean
to love you
with a
broken
heart
either.

We promised forever;
but sometimes,

forever
is just
a moment.

When they ask me
about true love,
I will tell them
about you.

But I will keep it a secret,
that even true love,
sometimes doesn't
last forever.

And if we ever meet again,
I hope your soul
remembers
the touch
 of my

     s o u l.

Dear reader,

Three years ago, I wouldn't have imagined I'd write poetry, much less share it with the world in the form of a poetry collection.

This book describes important aspects of my life and my writing journey, beginning with the first poem I ever wrote three years ago and spanning into some of my latest work. With each poem I write, I become a better writer.

Thank you for your never-ending support and for believing in me even on the days I don't believe in myself. I'm grateful for each inspiring poet I've met on my journey and for every reader who gives my words a home.
I hope to meet many more.

"Never give up on any dream."

~ Love, Ginnie

Give your heart time to heal ♥